Peaks and Valleys: Poems about Mental Health

Kelsey Senecker

Presentation by *BookLeaf Publishing*

Web: www.bookleafpub.com

E-mail: info@bookleafpub.com

ISBN: 9789363314344

First edition 2024

*To my parents, who have loved and encouraged
me through everything. Thank you so much.*

PREFACE

Please be advised, these poems may deal with
intense or difficult topics.

Declaration

I'd rather you stand upon a mountain
And scream THIS SUITS ME ILL
Than go alone in winter
And lose you to the chill.
Don't deny yourself a lifeboat
Do seek shelter from the storm
Please don't set yourself on fire
Just to keep another warm.
It doesn't matter the method
I'll always want to help
So whether song or sign or siren
Don't be afraid to give a yelp.

Masking

Whenever someone calls
I laugh and say I'm fine
And when it's a harder haul
I'm still in my right mind
Even though I'm trembling
When no one else can see
And something quite resembling
A panic's inside of me.
I'd rather be the one upset
Just me instead of you
Although in the end I suspect
Even that will not be true.

Depression

Oozing, creeping, scrabbling
Crepuscular sludge,
That leaks in through the cracks,
Stinking, sticking, staining
Strangling heart and brain and lung,
Hungering, slavering, craving
For hope and emotion's meat
Lurking, prowling, trailing
Until it strikes – and feasts.

Anxiety

A scuttling, crawling feeling
That creeps along the spine,
A time where crowds turn and stare
As though I've lost my mind,
A leaden, colossal boulder
Sitting squarely in my chest,
Days where I weep and sleep
But never emerge refreshed,
Nights where brains go and go
Yet still spin within the murk,
Stretches where nothing happens
But it sits in mind and lurks.

Bad OCD Day

Slice, scratch, bash, repeat,
Head and hands and spine and feet
Twice a second, ten thousand an hour,
Slice, scratch, bash, repeat.

A corrosive storm that erodes willpower
A rumbling that makes logic cower
Slice, scratch, bash, repeat.

Working, resting, in the shower,
Feeling bright or feeling dour:
Slice, scratch, bash, repeat.

Fear and guilt make moments sour
As echoes all my time devour:
Head and hands and spine and feet,
Slice, scratch, bash, repeat.

Panic attack

Too much too much too much – can't breathe –
too much too much
Bone-tight skin over sharp shapes lungs of stone
blood burning pathways from here to unknowns
– can't breathe can't breathe can't breathe can't
breathe
I close my eyes as my hands shake as my
shoulders shake as my body shakes
Need to run hide get away don't touch me don't
touch me I'll shatter
Someone is speaking to me, counting breaths
(Breathe for me, for me please)
It comes in gasps, that breath, and the voice
drones on (Please breathe)
I cannot stand but cannot sit still gasping, eyes
open eyes shut eyes open
The world is stabbing at me too loud too cold
too hot too something something I cannot name
but can feel like a wounded animal
A wounded animal in a trap gnawing and
gnawing and gnawing and (Please breathe, for
me, for me) some sort of count but it doesn't fit
Help me please don't touch me it's too much too
much too much
I can't think.

Breathe

In,
Out.
Feel it fill your chest,
Let it expand your belly
And softly flow out again.
Let the gentle pressure and release ground you
Bring you back from the spiral
Back from the abyss
And back to yourself here.

Remember:
In,
Out.
In,
Out.

Love

I'd spent so many nights pulling inward
Terrified to show anyone
How dark my thoughts had become,
Convinced the best way to endure
Was to travel on alone.
But my aching soul was breaking,
My battered heart straining,
My brain barely clinging to life.
So I stumbled towards her sleeping form,
Shaking hands finally serving a purpose,
And begged for a minute, a moment,
A nanosecond of sitting together against the
void.
I expected a mumble, a maybe later,
A not right now or a never,
But instead she rubbed the sleep from her eyes,
Cleared the crack from her voice,
And, rising, said
"I'm here for you."
"How can I help?"

This is Not for You

This is not for you
These long dark days where the sun doesn't
shine
And bright bright nights where all you can do
Is rock back and forth with your head and arms
in your knees
And whisper
I'm so tired
I don't know
I'm so tired
I don't know
As all around you your flaws stand out as stark
mountains –
The only thing for eons –
Positivity seeming to only be a vaporous and
forgotten dream,
Too fragile to even bring to mind.
And to stay in these trenches is far crueler than
any god would have the right to ask
So please remember that this is not for you.
I reach out a trembling hand now
And beg you to take it
Please take it
I want to help even though you may think
That it's not worth it

That you're not worth it
That the only justice in the world would be to
sink into the mud at your feet
Churned up by so much blood and sweat and
tears
And vanish into the never was.
Please take my hand
This is not for you
And it was not for me
When I laid sobbing in the depths of my own,
Convinced that the only way out was further
down
That misery was all I'd ever own and all I'd ever
deserved
And that only oblivion could rob me of my
sorrow.
This is not for you or me or us
Or anyone.

The way out will be hard
And progress is not always linear
So some part of you may look back for a while
yet
And think you should stay here.
I cannot promise it will be easy even to myself
But it will be harder alone,
And if I can't justify giving myself the gift of
grace
Perhaps we can extend it to each other

As we stumble out of the pit
Holding hands and whispering
This is not for you.

Knowledge

Lost in a mist of maybes
And haunted by my tears,
I staggered into an office
Desperate to know what was wrong.
Many nights of turmoil
Shook my hands and voice
I cleared my throat and whispered
"Where do I belong?"
The doctor spoke so calmly,
Assuaging all my fears
The packet lay between us,
Such a simple, quiet thing,
Yet in my mind so weighty
As it listed what she'd seen.
We went through it slowly
And my heart began to sing.
I was only battered,
Not broken, not destroyed
My monsters had a name
And could be beaten back!
I knew it wouldn't be easy
But at least it was a start
I now had a suit of armor,
And could press on with my attack.

Comorbidities

In 1610, Galileo puts an eye to his telescope and focuses
On a world other than our own,
Discovering around Jupiter
The first moon known beyond Earth's.
In time almost a hundred will be discovered,
A system that revolutionizes our understanding
of the universe.

Modern day brings me to an office
Where a doctor focuses
Her telescope-tests on my personal planet,
Examining it for orbits peculiar,
Orbits different from the known.
What she finds revolutionizes my understanding
Of myself and my place in the world.
My brain sports not one, but a few satellites,
A thing not uncommon, the doctor said.
Oftentimes when one brain-moon is found,
Multiple are.

Mourning

For days unlived
And nights gone by
And maybe-might-have-beens,
For things that in your times of youth
Were certain would come true.
For a world of sights unseen
Forced away by cloudy skies
For all the times that didn't occur
And those that did instead:
It is okay to weep and mourn
In lieu of shaking head.

Healing

The first thing to know about healing
Is that you won't always see it.
Some days, you're on top of the world
And others the world is battering down your
door
Screaming that you're a monster, a villain,
A wretch and a devil.
This is to be expected.
The path to healing is not always straight
Not always directly from A,
To B,
To C:
Sometimes it's more like a scribbled snarl
A line that takes ages to untangle,
And even longer to traverse.
This is ok.
Remind yourself that even if it's not linear,
Your effort matters
And every day you are still around
Is another victory yet.

Steady Effort

In order to move a mountain
You need to start with sand
Wear it away, bit by bit
Until the boulders come in view.
Then take that persistent effort
And grind them down to gravel.
You don't need a trebuchet,
Just determination's power;
The cracks will show, slow but sure
And the mountain will unravel.

Change Comes Softly

When winter seems to linger
Far longer than it ought,
When days are grey and dreary
And always tinged with frost,
When it seems that times like summer
Will forever stay away,
When your house is tuck in snowdrifts
Til it seems the end of May –
Remember gentle snowdrops
Will bloom despite the chill,
And though it seems summer never comes
Know that spring someday will.

Strength

When asked "What is strength?"
Someone might respond
With Superman or Lasha Talakhadze
Or maybe Deontay Wilder.
And these people are strong, no doubt.
But there's also a different kind of strength,
A quiet strength,
In facing down the dark,
In choosing to stay day after day
And night after night
Despite the devils that whisper in the void.
Strength isn't just bulging muscles
And world records
And medals:
It's also found
In the person who spent all night crying
Convinced they've never been worth anything
And never will be,
Now taking life one second at a time
In the hopes that something,
Anything,
Will prove them wrong.
If that is you,
Know that you are among the strongest people
That I've ever heard of
And that will never change.

Ways to Help

Figuring out how to help can be hard.
It's easy to assume it must be grand gestures,
Lavish, awe-inspiring, magnificent.
But the best assistance I have ever received
Was quite simple.
A patient ear when my brain wouldn't slow
down,
A solid hug when all I could do was cry,
A calm companion when I was scared to be
alone.
From the outside,
These may seem small.
But to a suffering friend,
They can be exactly what they need.

Stigma

Blurring the lines of the self is never easy
But sometimes I look in a person's eyes
And know it must be done,
Know they won't accept "Harm OCD"
And maybe not even "OCD"
Nor "Depression," nor "Anxiety,"
That any mental illness is foreign,
Is other,
Is terrifying.
So I fold myself inwards,
Ignoring the pain that comes with it,
Trying not to be a monster.

Progress

From foreign fey child
To forgotten and institutionalized
To mental health awareness month,
Much has changed over the centuries.
Often it was through lots
And lots
Of excruciating effort,
But it is progress yet.
And though there is still a long way to go,
One look at how far we've come,
One thought of all the past fighters cheering us
on,
One inkling of how grand it could be,
Is enough to fill me with hope.

Tomorrow Needs You

Tomorrow needs you.
Your sparkle,
Your spirit,
Your specific special spin
On this world of wanderers.
Tomorrow needs You.
Your neighbor won't do
And neither would your aunt,
Or your friend or anyone else at all.
Even though you may not see it,
Today is richer for your presence
And it would be a shame
To deprive tomorrow of that milieu.
Tomorrow Needs You.

1 in 8

In the bleak black of numbness
And the rigid white of anxiety
It's easy to feel isolated,
Single, solitary, alone.
Who else could be so wrong
Your brain whispers
So flawed, so faulty,
Responsible for all the world's sins?
Surely no one else but you.
The voice sneaks in deeper
Spilling tales of blame and delinquency,
Of trespass and atrocity,
Perhaps even suggesting a solution or two:
A simple thing, a deadly thing,
And the edges of your vision grey.

But from across the void comes calling
A softer, sweeter song:
1 in 8 the world around,
You're not alone, you belong.
Don't let the doubts that linger
Take you forever from the day
1 in 8, the world around
We shall never fade away!

www.ingramcontent.com/pod-product-compliance
Lightning Source LLC
LaVergne TN
LVHW010856200726

843508LV00012B/2917